DOG BREEDS

Pomeranians

by Sara Green

Consultant:
Michael Leuthner, D.V.M.
Petcare Animal Hospital
Madison, Wisc.

BLASTOFF! READERS
4

BELLWETHER MEDIA · MINNEAPOLIS, MN

Note to Librarians, Teachers, and Parents:

Blastoff! Readers are carefully developed by literacy experts and combine standards-based content with developmentally appropriate text.

Level 1 provides the most support through repetition of high-frequency words, light text, predictable sentence patterns, and strong visual support.

Level 2 offers early readers a bit more challenge through varied simple sentences, increased text load, and less repetition of high-frequency words.

Level 3 advances early-fluent readers toward fluency through increased text and concept load, less reliance on visuals, longer sentences, and more literary language.

Level 4 builds reading stamina by providing more text per page, increased use of punctuation, greater variation in sentence patterns, and increasingly challenging vocabulary.

Level 5 encourages children to move from "learning to read" to "reading to learn" by providing even more text, varied writing styles, and less familiar topics.

Whichever book is right for your reader, Blastoff! Readers are the perfect books to build confidence and encourage a love of reading that will last a lifetime!

This edition first published in 2011 by Bellwether Media, Inc.

No part of this publication may be reproduced in whole or in part without written permission of the publisher. For information regarding permission, write to Bellwether Media, Inc., Attention: Permissions Department, 5357 Penn Avenue South, Minneapolis, MN 55419.

Library of Congress Cataloging-in-Publication Data
Green, Sara, 1964–
Pomeranians / by Sara Green.
    p. cm. — (Blastoff! readers. Dog breeds)
Includes bibliographical references and index.
    Summary: "Simple text and full-color photographs introduce beginning readers to the characteristics of the dog breed Pomeranians. Developed by literacy experts for students in kindergarten through third grade"—Provided by publisher.
ISBN 978-1-60014-567-4 (hardcover : alk. paper)
1. Pomeranian dog–Juvenile literature. I. Title.
SF429.P8G745 2011
636.76–dc22   2010034491

Printed in the United States of America, North Mankato, MN.
010111   1176

Contents

What Are Pomeranians?

Pomeranians are small dogs with thick **coats** and long, fluffy tails. People often call them Poms. The Pomeranian **breed** is a member of the **Toy Group** of dogs.

Adult Pomeranians weigh between 3 and 7 pounds (1 and 3 kilograms). They are 7 to 12 inches (18 to 30 centimeters) tall at the shoulder.

! fun fact

The 26th President of the United States, Theodore Roosevelt, owned a Pomeranian named Gem.

Pomeranians have **double coats**. The short, dense undercoat keeps Pomeranians warm in cold weather. The long, straight hairs of the outer coat are called **guard hairs**. They help keep the undercoat clean and dry. Pomeranian coats come in many colors. The most common are orange, white, black, and **parti-color**.

parti-color

! fun fact

Female Pomeranians are often slightly larger than male Pomeranians.

Pomeranians have small, pointed ears that sit high on their heads. Their **muzzles** are short and straight.

Pomeranians have bushy tails that curl over their backs. Some Pomeranians have tails that curl all the way up to their heads!

History of Pomeranians

Spitz dog

Pomeranians come from the Spitz family of dogs. Spitz dogs are known for their good health and ability to endure harsh weather. They are common in northern and central Europe.

For hundreds of years, people used Spitz dogs as **sled dogs**. In a region of northern Europe called Pomerania, people began keeping small Spitz dogs as **companion dogs**.

In the 1700s and 1800s, the royal family of England brought these small Spitz dogs from Pomerania to England. The dogs became known as Pomeranians. Queen Victoria liked little Pomeranians. In the late 1800s, she had a Pomeranian named Marco.

Queen Victoria

Many people wanted a dog like the Queen's. People chose the smallest Pomeranians to have puppies. In time, all Pomeranians were tiny.

Pomeranians came to the United States in the late 1800s. Their fluffy look and friendly nature made them popular pets. Their **instinct** to bark at strangers also made people choose them as **watchdogs**.

Pomeranians Today

Pomeranians are very intelligent and enjoy challenging activities. Many Pomeranians do well in **obedience trials**. In these events, owners command their dogs to sit, stay, and come. Judges give points to dogs that follow the commands correctly. The dog that follows the commands the best wins.

fun fact

A Pomeranian is called a *Zwergspitz* in Germany. The German words *Zwerg* and *spitz* mean "dwarf" and "pointed." Pomeranians are small dogs with pointed ears!

Pomeranians also participate in physical challenges. Many Pomeranians and their owners compete in **Teacup Agility**. In this sport, small dogs run through a course of tunnels, ramps, and other obstacles. The dog that finishes fastest and with the fewest mistakes is the winner!

Pomeranians love to play at home. They like to chase balls outside, but they are also happy playing indoors with their owners.

Pomeranians are loyal to their families and friends. They may be small, but their personalities are big enough to win anyone over!

Glossary

breed—a type of dog

coats—the hair or fur of animals

companion dogs—dogs that provide friendship to people

double coats—the coats of animals that have both an outer coat and an undercoat

guard hairs—the long, straight hairs of the outer coat

instinct—a natural way to behave without being taught

muzzles—the noses, jaws, and mouths of animals

obedience trials—events where dogs perform commands from their owners in front of judges

parti-color—having two solid colors; one of the colors must be white.

sled dogs—dogs used to pull sleds in snow

Teacup Agility—a sport for small dogs where they run through a series of obstacles

Toy Group—a group of dog breeds that weigh less than 10 pounds (4.5 kilograms)

watchdogs—dogs trained to keep watch over property; watchdogs bark if they see strangers.

To Learn More

AT THE LIBRARY
American Kennel Club. *The Complete Dog Book for Kids*. New York, N.Y.: Howell Book House, 1996.

Baker, Olga. *Pomeranian*. Allenhurst, N.J.: Kennel Club Books, 2005.

Gray, Susan H. *Pomeranians*. Mankato, Minn.: Child's World, 2008.

ON THE WEB
Learning more about Pomeranians is as easy as 1, 2, 3.

1. Go to www.factsurfer.com.

2. Enter "Pomeranians" into the search box.

3. Click the "Surf" button and you will see a list of related Web sites.

With factsurfer.com, finding more information is just a click away.

Index

The images in this book are reproduced through the courtesy of: Suponev Vladimir, front cover; Juan Martinez, pp. 4-5, 8, 14-15, 21; Juniors Bildarchiv, p. 6 (small); Mark Raycroft/Getty Images, pp. 6-7; Faith A. Uridel/KimballStock, p. 9; Juniors Bildarchiv/Age Fotostock, p. 10; Jon Eppard, p. 11; Wikipedia, p. 12 (small); pixshots, pp. 12-13; Daniel Hernandez, pp. 16-17; Dempster Dogs/Alamy, pp. 18-19, 19 (small); J. Harrison/KimballStock, p. 20.